Nutrition

Water

by Susan Glick

FOCUS READERS

BEACON

www.focusreaders.com

Focus Readers is distributed by North Star Editions:
sales@northstareditions.com | 888-417-0195

Produced for Focus Readers by Red Line Editorial.

Photographs ©: Shutterstock Images, cover, 1, 4, 6, 8, 11, 13, 14–15, 19, 20, 22, 26; iStockphoto, 16, 25, 29

Library of Congress Cataloging-in-Publication Data
Names: Glick, Susan, author.
Title: Water / by Susan Glick.
Description: Mendota Heights, MN : Focus Readers, [2025] | Series: Nutrition | Includes bibliographical references and index. | Audience: Grades 2-3
Identifiers: LCCN 2023053157 (print) | LCCN 2023053158 (ebook) | ISBN 9798889981862 (hardcover) | ISBN 9798889982425 (paperback) | ISBN 9798889983521 (pdf) | ISBN 9798889982982 (ebook)
Subjects: LCSH: Water in the body--Juvenile literature. | Dehydration (Physiology)--Juvenile literature. | Nutrition--Juvenile literature.
Classification: LCC QP535.H1 G55 2025 (print) | LCC QP535.H1 (ebook) | DDC 612/.01522--dc23/eng/20231229
LC record available at https://lccn.loc.gov/2023053157
LC ebook record available at https://lccn.loc.gov/2023053158

Printed in the United States of America
Mankato, MN
082024

About the Author

Susan Glick lives in Maryland, where she writes books for children.

Table of Contents

Chapter 1

Drink Up

A girl wakes up early. She drinks a big glass of water. Then she goes to school. During history class, she sips from her water bottle. After science class, she fills the bottle at a water fountain.

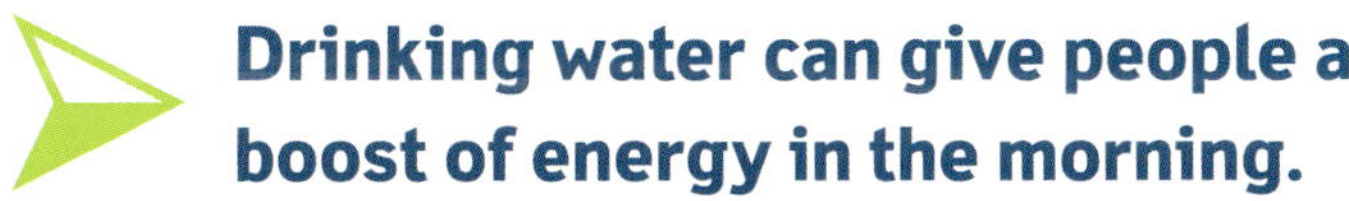

Exercise can cause people to feel more thirsty.

The girl drinks throughout the day. She gives her body plenty of water. She knows it is important to stay **hydrated**.

After school, the girl has a soccer game. It is a hot afternoon. So, she drinks lots of water during breaks. By halftime, her water bottle is empty. Her coach refills it with a big jug of water.

The team wins! Afterward, the girl eats a slice of juicy watermelon with her teammates. The healthy snack has more of the water her body needs.

Chapter 2

We Need Water

Humans need water to stay healthy. Water is in every part of the body. It helps the body do important jobs. For example, water is in cells. It helps them break down chemicals and **nutrients**.

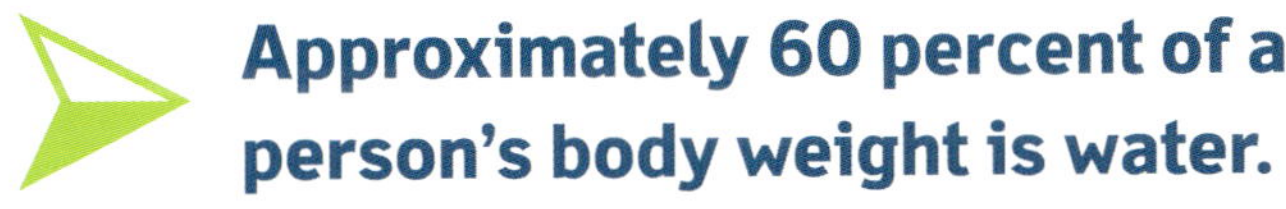

Approximately 60 percent of a person's body weight is water.

Water has other uses in the body. Blood is mostly made of water. Water helps blood move freely to cells. That way, blood can transport nutrients and **oxygen** around the body.

Water is also in bones. It acts like a cushion between them. Water protects the **spine**. It also helps joints, such as elbows and knees, bend easily.

Water helps keep the body cool, too. This often happens when a

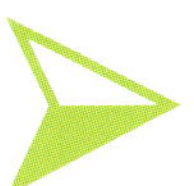

Drinking water helps keep a cushion around the spine. Not drinking enough can cause back pain.

person exercises. It also happens when a person is hot. Water leaves the body as sweat. Sweat keeps the body from overheating.

Water is also an important part of **digestion**. Water helps break down food. It frees up nutrients in the food. Then water helps move waste out of the body. Water also helps kidneys clean blood. This waste leaves the body in urine.

The body loses some of its water every day. So, it is important to

Water helps **muscles** work properly. Without it, they cannot move as well.

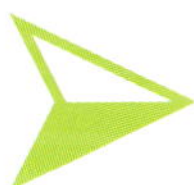
Not getting enough water can cause headaches.

replenish it by drinking often. Different people need different amounts of water. It depends on how much exercise a person gets. It also depends on the temperature.

A CLOSER LOOK

Dehydration

Dehydration is when the body does not have the water it needs. It can happen when a person forgets to drink. Or it can happen when a person sweats a lot. Dehydration may also happen when a person is sick. Vomiting makes the body lose water. So does diarrhea.

Dehydrated people may feel very thirsty. They might stop urinating. They may feel dizzy or confused. The only way to help is to put more water into the body. People can drink water or get it from an **IV**.

The body may lose up to 1 gallon (4 L) of water per hour in sweat.

Chapter 3

Good Choices

The best way to stay hydrated is to drink plain water. It has no **calories**. And it can be found in many places. However, other drinks can help people stay hydrated, too.

Sparkling water and seltzers are healthy drink options.

Unsweetened milk is one healthy option. All kinds of milk contain water. Plus, milk can be a good source of calcium and vitamin D. Smoothies made from fruits and vegetables are another good choice. Some ingredients may add nutrients. But it is important to limit sugar.

People can also get water from the food they eat. Fruits and berries are excellent sources. Many are made mostly of water. Plus, they provide other kinds of nutrients.

Strawberries are approximately 91 percent water.

Vegetables also have water. In fact, some vegetables contain even more water than fruits. Lettuce and cucumbers are good options. So are bean sprouts.

Sugary drinks can harm the liver, heart, and kidneys.

People should avoid drinks that have lots of added sugar. Lemonade and soda are two examples. Energy drinks are another. These drinks are high in calories. They are also bad for teeth. Diet sodas with sugar **substitutes** are also bad for health.

Sports drinks and fruit juices may seem healthy, but they often have lots of added sugars. People who have lots of sugary drinks are more likely to get certain diseases.

A can of soda may contain more than 10 teaspoons (40 g) of sugar.

DRIN
A GLAS
OF WATER

Chapter 4

Healthy Habits

Experts suggest drinking water throughout the day. The amount a person needs can change. People should drink whenever they feel thirsty. It can be a good idea to drink a glass with each meal.

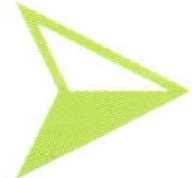

Using alarms or other reminders can help a person remember to drink water.

Using a refillable water bottle is a great way to keep water close by. It also reduces waste from plastic bottles. Drinking from a water fountain is another way to stay hydrated.

Some people like flavored water. There are ways to change the flavor without added sugars. Berries or orange slices can give water a fruity taste. Cucumber or mint can give water a refreshing taste. A splash of fruit juice can add flavor, too.

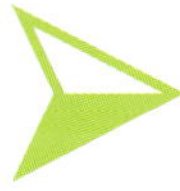

Refillable water bottles can help people keep track of how much water they drink.

Drinking different kinds of unsweetened milk can also help. That includes cow's milk. It also includes milks made from almonds, oats, or soy. But milk should not be a person's only source of water.

Soups and broths can be good sources of water.

Eating a variety of foods is another way to help the body get the water it needs. Nearly all foods contain some water. Eating salads and fruits can be a good way to stay hydrated.

People should pay attention to when the body needs extra water. For example, they may need to drink extra water on hot days. They may also need to drink more water when they're sick. The body works best when it gets the water it needs.

People get 20 percent of the water they need from food.

FOCUS ON
Water

Write your answers on a separate piece of paper.

1. Write a few sentences describing the different ways the body uses water.
2. Which healthy source of water do you like best? Why?
3. Which of the following drinks is a healthy source of water?
   A. a sports drink
   B. fruit juice
   C. unsweetened milk
4. What might happen if a person did not drink extra water on a hot day?
   A. The person might get dehydrated.
   B. The person might not feel thirsty.
   C. The person might feel very cold.

5. What does **transport** mean in this book?

*Water helps blood move freely to cells. That way, blood can **transport** nutrients and oxygen around the body.*

A. to take something from one place to another
B. to watch something very closely
C. to add something to a mixture

6. What does **replenish** mean in this book?

*The body loses some of its water every day. So, it is important to **replenish** it by drinking often.*

A. pay attention to
B. fill up again
C. ignore or forget

Answer key on page 32.

Glossary

calories
Units that describe how much energy the body can get from a food or drink.

digestion
The process of breaking down food so it can be used by the body.

hydrated
Supplied with water.

IV
A tube that delivers fluid or medicine into a vein. The letters *IV* are short for *intravenous*.

muscles
Parts of the body that help with strength and movement.

nutrients
Substances that living things need to stay strong and healthy.

oxygen
A gas in the air that humans and animals need to breathe to survive.

spine
A set of bones that holds up the back and protects nerves.

substitutes
Things that are used in place of other things.

To Learn More

BOOKS

Koster, Gloria. *Water Is Good for You*. North Mankato, MN: Capstone Press, 2023.

Rea, Amy C. *Water as a Necessary Nutrient*. Minneapolis: Abdo Publishing, 2023.

Rebman, Nick. *Earth-Friendly Eating*. Mendota Heights, MN: Focus Readers, 2022.

NOTE TO EDUCATORS

Visit **www.focusreaders.com** to find lesson plans, activities, links, and other resources related to this title.

Index

Answer Key: 1. Answers will vary; **2.** Answers will vary; **3.** C; **4.** A; **5.** A; **6.** B